DIGGING UP THE PAST

ROSETTA STONE

BY TRUDY BECKER

WWW.APEXEDITIONS.COM

Copyright © 2026 by Apex Editions, Mendota Heights, MN 55120. All rights reserved. No part of this book may be reproduced or utilized in any form or by any means without written permission from the publisher.

Apex is distributed by North Star Editions:
sales@northstareditions.com | 888-417-0195

Produced for Apex by Red Line Editorial.

Photographs ©: Shutterstock Images, cover, 1, 6–7, 12, 13, 15, 16–17, 22–23, 24, 26, 27, 29; iStockphoto, 4–5, 9, 10–11, 18; Marie-Lan Nguyen/Louvre Museum, 14; Art Media/Print Collector/Hulton Archive/Getty Images, 19; Florilegius/Alamy, 21; The British Museum, 25

Library of Congress Control Number: 2025930919

ISBN
979-8-89250-535-2 (hardcover)
979-8-89250-571-0 (paperback)
979-8-89250-641-0 (ebook pdf)
979-8-89250-607-6 (hosted ebook)

Printed in the United States of America
Mankato, MN
082025

NOTE TO PARENTS AND EDUCATORS

Apex books are designed to build literacy skills in striving readers. Exciting, high-interest content attracts and holds readers' attention. The text is carefully leveled to allow students to achieve success quickly. Additional features, such as bolded glossary words for difficult terms, help build comprehension.

CHAPTER 1
A STONE IN THE SAND 4

CHAPTER 2
ABOUT THE STONE 10

CHAPTER 3
BREAKING THE CODE 16

CHAPTER 4
FURTHER LEARNING 22

COMPREHENSION QUESTIONS • 28
GLOSSARY • 30
TO LEARN MORE • 31
ABOUT THE AUTHOR • 31
INDEX • 32

CHAPTER 1

A STONE IN THE SAND

In 1799, a group of French soldiers work on a hot day. They are fighting in northern Egypt. They are making a **fort** stronger.

Napoleon Bonaparte led France in the late 1700s and early 1800s. In 1798, he attacked Egypt.

The soldiers take down an old stone wall. They find a large, dark stone. They try to move it. But it is too heavy to lift.

FAST FACT

The dark stone weighed 1,676 pounds (760 kg).

Soldiers found the stone near the Nile River. This river flows north through Egypt.

The soldiers brush away dirt. They uncover more of the dark stone. It is covered in writing. It shows three different **scripts**. All are from long ago. It becomes known as the Rosetta Stone.

EXTRA COPIES

In 1801, British forces defeated the French in Egypt. The British took the stone. But the French had made copies. They kept studying these versions.

The Rosetta Stone has three types of writing carved into its surface.

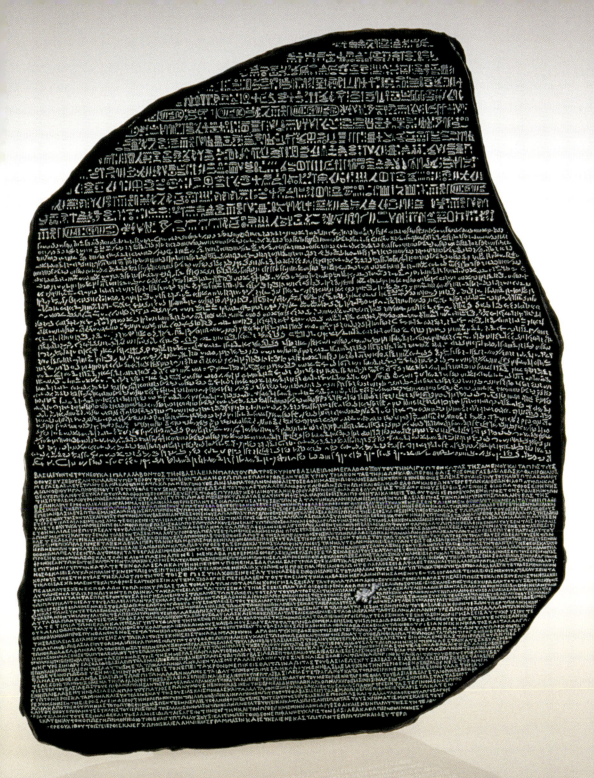

CHAPTER 2

About the Stone

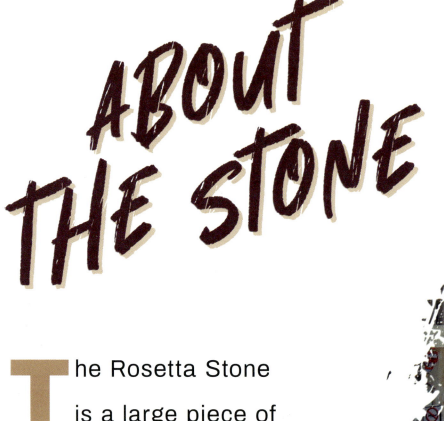

The Rosetta Stone is a large piece of black rock. It stands about 44 inches (112 cm) tall. Soldiers found it in Rashīd, Egypt.

The city of Rashīd is sometimes called Rosetta. That's how the stone got its name.

The Rosetta Stone is a piece of a larger rock. Other parts broke off and have not been found.

The top of the stone has **hieroglyphs**. The middle uses Demotic. That is a simple way of writing in ancient Egyptian. And ancient Greek covers the bottom.

DIFFERENT LANGUAGES

Many people moved into and out of ancient Egypt. Egyptians also traded with faraway nations. So, Egyptians used a few different languages. That's why the stone had three types of writing.

Ancient Egyptians often used Demotic script to write books, letters, or business documents.

At first, **scholars** could read only the Greek part. But they also knew Coptic. That language is **related** to Demotic. It helped them **decipher** some of the Demotic. But the hieroglyphs were a mystery.

Coptic was an Egyptian language. But it used the Greek alphabet.

Egyptian hieroglyphs use more than 700 shapes and symbols.

FAST FACT

The Greek text said all three scripts gave the same message.

CHAPTER 3

BREAKING THE CODE

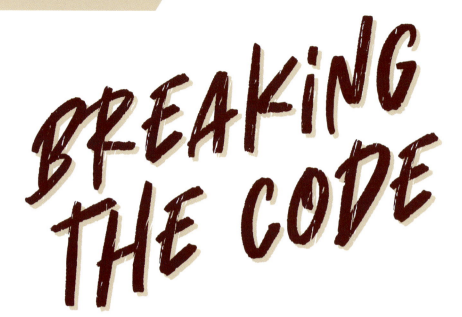

Scholars found names in the Greek writing. They searched for those names in the other scripts. In the 1810s, Thomas Young did this. He found hieroglyphs for the name "Ptolemy."

In both Demotic and hieroglyphic writing, people's names are circled.

Jean-François Champollion studied the Rosetta Stone for 14 years.

French scholar Jean-François Champollion made another find in 1822. He figured out the sounds that some hieroglyphs stood for. That helped him unlock many more hieroglyphs.

SOUNDING IT OUT

Champollion figured out the name "Ramses." This name had four hieroglyphs. One was used twice. It stood for the "s" sound. Another was a circle and dot. It stood for "ra."

Champollion wrote notes about the symbols and sounds he figured out.

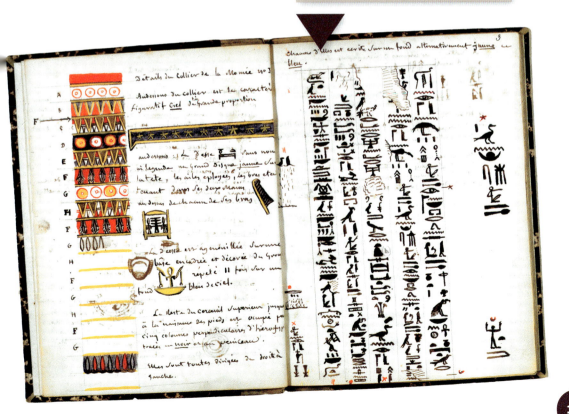

People could finally read all three parts of the stone. Each script repeated a **decree**. It was from 196 BCE. It celebrated Egypt's king.

FAST FACT
The king's name was Ptolemy V Epiphanes. He ruled from 205 to 180 BCE.

The Rosetta Stone described how Egypt would honor King Ptolemy V Epiphanes.

CHAPTER 4

FURTHER LEARNING

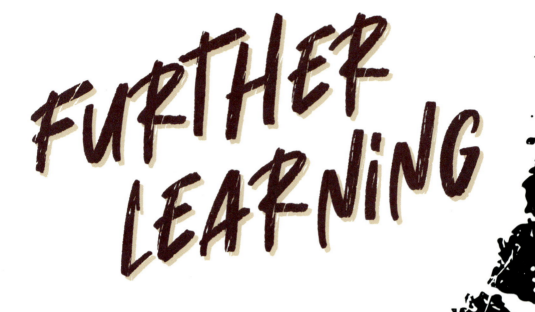

The Rosetta Stone helped scholars learn about ancient Egypt. In the decree, a group of priests listed good things the king had done. They promised **loyalty** to him.

Egyptian kings were called pharaohs. They were said to be sons of the sun god, Ra.

Hieroglyphs cover the walls of many ancient Egyptian temples and monuments.

Scholars could now read other hieroglyphs, too. They translated ancient texts. And they read writings found in temples and tombs.

PAST KINGS

In 1820, researchers found lists of Egyptian kings. Reading these lists showed how old ancient Egypt was. The first king began ruling around 3150 BCE.

Some scholars read the *Book of the Dead*. They learned what ancient Egyptians believed about life after death.

Egyptology is the study of ancient Egypt. Egyptologists may study the ruins of old pyramids and temples.

The Rosetta Stone sparked interest in Egypt. Many scholars traveled there. They studied ruins and old items. People learned more about the past.

FAST FACT
The Rosetta Stone sits in the British Museum in London, England.

Thousands of visitors see the Rosetta Stone every year. A glass case protects it.

COMPREHENSION QUESTIONS

Write your answers on a separate piece of paper.

1. Write a few sentences explaining the main points of Chapter 2.

2. Would you like to learn how to read hieroglyphs? Why or why not?

3. When was the Rosetta Stone found?
   - A. 1799
   - B. 1801
   - C. 1822

4. How might trading with faraway nations shape how Egyptians used language?
   - A. Egyptians wouldn't need to read or write.
   - B. Egyptians might learn the languages those nations used.
   - C. Egyptians might talk only with people from those nations.

5. What does **versions** mean in this book?

*But the French had made copies. They kept studying these **versions**.*

    A. new types of food
    B. new forms of an earlier thing
    C. very large buildings

6. What does **translated** mean in this book?

*Scholars could now read other hieroglyphs, too. They **translated** ancient texts. And they read writings found in temples and tombs.*

    A. broke something into many pieces
    B. changed something from one language to another
    C. changed the name of a person

Answer key on page 32.

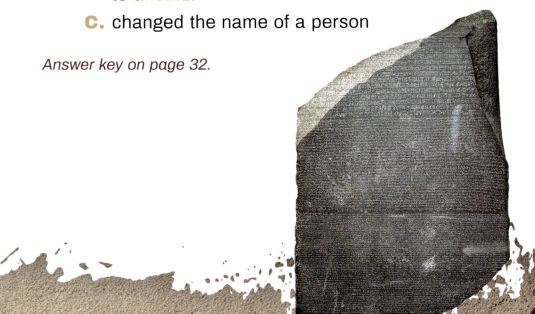

GLOSSARY

decipher
To figure out the meaning of something.

decree
An official order, often sent out by a ruler.

fort
A strong building used to watch over and protect an area.

hieroglyphs
Pictures that represent words or sounds in the ancient Egyptian language.

loyalty
Strong support for a person or thing.

related
Coming from the same older language and having some traits in common as a result.

scholars
People who spend lots of time and effort studying something.

scripts
Sets of letters or characters that are used to write a language.

TO LEARN MORE

BOOKS

Doeden, Matt. *Travel to Egypt*. Lerner Publications, 2024.

Gieseke, Tyler. *Egyptian Gods and Goddesses.* Abdo Publishing, 2022.

Murray, Julie. *King Tut's Tomb*. Abdo Publishing, 2022.

ONLINE RESOURCES

Visit **www.apexeditions.com** to find links and resources related to this title.

ABOUT THE AUTHOR

Trudy Becker lives in Minneapolis, Minnesota. When she was a kid, she had a puzzle of the Rosetta Stone. She loved trying to decipher it.

INDEX

B
British Museum, 27
British soldiers, 8

C
Champollion, Jean-François, 18–19
Coptic, 14

D
Demotic, 12, 14

F
French soldiers, 4, 6, 8, 10

G
Greek, 12, 14–15, 16

H
hieroglyphs, 12, 14, 16, 18–19, 24

L
London, England, 27

P
Ptolemy V Epiphanes, 16, 20

R
Rashīd, Egypt, 10

S
scholars, 14, 16, 18, 22, 24, 26
scripts, 8, 15, 16, 20

Y
Young, Thomas, 16

ANSWER KEY:
1. Answers will vary; 2. Answers will vary; 3. A; 4. B; 5. B; 6. B